WRESTLING IN THE SPIRIT

Proverb 3:1-8

Prophet Elijah Dixon Jr

Copyright © 2016 by Prophet Elijah Dixon Jr

Wrestling in the Spirit
Proverb 3:1-8
by Prophet Elijah Dixon Jr

Printed in the United States of America.

ISBN 9781498471787

All rights reserved solely by the author. The author guarantees all contents are original and do not infringe upon the legal rights of any other person or work. No part of this book may be reproduced in any form without the permission of the author. The views expressed in this book are not necessarily those of the publisher.

www.xulonpress.com

Chapter 1

I always wondered *why me*; I was all alone. During my childhood years, I was not sure about myself. I would hide myself from other people who were not my family. I was born June 9, 1972 in Newberry, South Carolina. I was born with deformed arms, both being short with no wrists. I was not able to make a fist. My arms were both bound backward, and I would have multiple surgeries on both of them throughout my childhood. They had to break both arms to straighten them out with pins. It was terrible growing up with two deformed arms. People were always looking and staring at me. I just wanted to wear long-sleeved shirts all the time, but people were going to say something anyway; I thought I might as well be free. So as you see, I had a very different life from the beginning.

Swansea is a small town in South Carolina. With a population of about 827 people at the time, it was a small rural town outside of the capital city, which is Columbia. In Swansea there was no mall, hospital, skating rink, or city bus; we had no fast food restaurants and only one stop light in the whole town. We walked all over town, and it seemed like everybody was a cousin. The highlight on Friday was watching *Miami Vice* and walking to Zippy Mart to get a cold Guzzler drink. Swansea had four schools at the time: elementary, intermediate, middle and high school. The high school was the main attraction in Swansea—it was a real sports town. Swansea was 90% black and 10% white, and race relations between blacks and white were terrible. It seemed to me that a lot of blacks were scared of whites. White people looked down on the blacks. I witnessed a lot of black and white fights—I was even in a few of them. I grew up not liking white people because of what I saw them do to our black people. Race relations were not what I thought they should have been.

Gaston was the next town over from Swansea where most of the white people lived. Gaston and Swansea were rivals. The white people in Gaston had schools, but not a high school, so their kids had to go to Swansea High School. There were fights and arguments all the time. The only time we had peace together was on the football field, baseball diamond, or wrestling mat. Not all whites were bad people. I had plenty of genuine white friends. Going to school was a big event because we had friends and had unity together as one. Even most of our teachers were white, so we had to depend on each other.

Growing up in the late seventies was amazing in some ways because it was such a simple life in Swansea. In my first memories, it was my dad, my mom, my one brother and myself, but later we were joined by my three sisters. We lived in the country; we started out poor from what I could see. We did not have nice things like other people I knew. I remember, when I was a small child, we had a small house with a tin roof. There was no inside plumbing, and instead we had to go to the outhouse to use the bathroom. My mom ran hot water in an iron tub and that was how we washed up. We had chickens, and hogs; we lived the real country life. My brother and I collected beer and soda cans and would cash in the cans for money. We did really well with that. All I wanted was a nice pair of shoes and some comfort, but I was treated well by my parents, and I knew they loved me.

I had my mom and dad, plus one brother and four sisters. My dad was a man who worked hard to provide for us. We always had food, shelter, and clothes. My mom was a stay-at-home mom. She was the rock that the family depended on. She cooked breakfast and dinner every day of my life. She washed our clothes. My mom was illiterate and could not read, so she would always to encourage us to read well and get a good education and graduate from high school. My mom was warm and sweet, and always tried to keep the family together. She stayed with my dad because she wanted us to grow up with a father at home—even though he was there, I still felt like he was gone.

My dad was a man of very few words. He made it to the 11th grade in school. He did not allow us to go hardly anywhere. We stayed home with my mom, we never visited friends or relatives. He even stopped my mom from visiting her family. We were a bit isolated. Meanwhile, my dad always went out and partied. He was a smoker and a drinker. My dad worked at a place called Nauseas wire plant where they stripped copper and made telephones. My dad was a lead supervisor and made good money, but he also sold weed on the side. My dad would bag the weed and go sell it. Sometimes people would come by the house and buy it. If he was not home, he left some bags at home and my mom would sell it for him to people. My dad and his friends would party on the weekend and drink and smoke weed. They played loud music and my brother, sisters, and I would have to stay in our rooms during the parties—we were not allowed out.

Growing up, I had numerous surgeries on my arms; my mom went with me all the time. I remember my dad going once. As a boy I asked my dad "why my arms are like this?" He simply replied, "there are people in the world worse than you." My inner thoughts were broken and shattered as a young person. I could not get any answers to my questions.

Life with my dad was not all bad. We had family trips to Myrtle Beach where we stayed at the beach house and had fun. My dad also took us to the pro wrestling match in Augusta, Georgia. Christmas time was good for my family and me. We got presents and nice things; one year, when I was seven, we even got a go-cart. I loved that go-cart so much I could not wait to come home to ride it. We had a good life compared to other people, but my worst Christmas was when my brother and I did not get anything, but my sister got presents.

We went to church sometimes, but my dad did not go at all. I never understood that. He would make us go to church, but he would never join us. I loved going to church and listening to the music and the Word of God being preached. It felt like, sometimes, the preacher was talking directly to me and staring at me. As a little boy, I did not understand a lot of things, and my parents did not have the answers I was looking for. Giving my life over to Jesus Christ was the answer I needed. God had to teach me the plan and, to this day, I am still learning. He chose me to be this way so I could help others through my experiences.

I had to grow up with people laughing at me and picking at me. It really motivated me to be strong. There is no way that I could have lasted this long without God. I had to learn to live with myself and be proud of who I am. This can apply to anyone out there, not just the disabled in body. I realize that everyone has some kind of disability.

I remember my first day of school: it was my first grade year and I was seven years old. I walked into the room, and all eyes were on me. All the other little kids looked and stared at me. My teacher was Mrs. Williams, a very polite lady. She acted like I was one of her regular students. She did not treat me any differently. As time went on, my classmates got used to seeing me. The more we were together the more we bonded. Still, there were some students in higher grades who were very cruel to me, making remarks about way my arms were. I did try not understand why they were picking on me. Sometimes after school, I would get mad and want to fight. I was determine to get my revenge on people picking on me in school. I was ready to fight to the end as long as I could. I hated when kids at school would makes jokes about my arms and laugh at me. At the time I felt like fight back was the answer. I started to build up a wall emotionally. No matter what I did, some of them would not accept me. They acted like I was trying to take something away from them.

I noticed at the age of eleven, certain things started to change. We were moving to a new house. My parents built a new house closer to our family. Up until then, I did not know much about my cousins or grandparents or aunts or uncles, but I started to see them more. I was in fifth grade and I had made some friends, but there were still people who picked on me. I knew I was different because people treated me that way. We played games at school, and sometimes I was picked, but other times I just went solo. I did have one friend and his name was Wayne Colter. I had known him since first grade, but it wasn't until fifth grade that we became good friends. Wayne had a crush on my sister Michelle. My sister and I were only one year apart, so she was in the sixth grade at the time.

You know how when you were young, you wrote girls to say you wanted them to be your girlfriend? My peers all had girlfriends, but I did not. I was upset because some of the guys tried to hook me up with a certain girl. She said she was not going to be my girlfriend because of my arms. I was destroyed and thought to myself *why me*? My brother and sisters came out right. I was always the odd ball; I was nothing. However, as the year went along, Wayne and I began to form a bond. He did not treat me like the others did. Even his mom treated me like I was her son as well.

This time in school was difficult for me. I did not know who I was and what my purpose was. The only time I felt good about myself was when we went to church. My parents would send us to the Mt. Pleasant church that was up the street from our house. I felt a connection with the presence of God, but I did not understand it at all. I had a sense of belonging. There was no judgment or pain; I just felt like a member of the body of Christ. One Sunday morning during service, it felt like the preacher was preaching directly to me. I remember the words that came out of his mouth. He said, "Come to Jesus. Give Him your heart and be saved." So as you can see, from a little boy I knew I was connected to Jesus Christ; I just did not know how.

One day Wayne and I were walking to the Zippy mart to get a soft drink. We saw this man on the comer dressed kind of funny. It looked like he had a robe on; you know the one pastors wear in church. He stopped us to tell us about Jesus Christ. Then he touched my hand and said, "Young man, is there anything you want the Lord to do for you?"

I said, "Yes sir, I want the Lord to heal my arms and make them right."

He said, "Ok," and began to pray for me. Afterwards, he said to me, "You know, you are going to be a preacher one day."

I looked at him and said, "Yes sir." I just took the man at his word and believed him that I would one day become a preacher of God's Word.

As we continued our walk to the store, we both looked back and the man was gone. There was no trace of the man. I saw my cousin Toby coming around the corner, so I asked him if he saw him, but he did not see anybody. From that day on, in the back of my mind I was curious about what the Lord had in store for me. That was our first encounter with an angel of the Lord.

Chapter 2

It was Wednesday afternoon and we were about to let out from school for Thanksgiving break. The bell rang and I thought *good, no more school for at least 4 days*. Wayne and I had most of all our classes together, and we walked to school along with the rest of the kids in the neighborhood. As we began to walk, I saw my sister Michelle walking with her friends. Everyone was laughing and talking loudly, excited for our break from school and all the fun Thanksgiving would surely bring.

Suddenly, we all heard a loud noise and I ran to the front to see what was going on.

"Michelle got hit by a car!" I heard someone scream.

Eric's sister is named Michelle too, I thought, *it could be her. Not my Shell.* Once I pushed my way to the front of the onlookers, I saw her. It was my sister. I was horrified. I started to run home. As I was running, I met my brother Anthony on the way and I told him. We ran home together as fast as we could.

"Mom!" I yelled, "Mom! Shell got hit by a car!"

She cried out. "When? Where?"

We told her everything we knew. Somehow, somebody got in contact with my dad while he was at work. My uncle Sonny Boy came over to take my mom where Shell was. Shell was hurt very badly and blood was coming out of her mouth. She was not moving at all. The ambulance was already at the site by the time my dad got there. They were trying to treat her, but they could not get a response, so they called in a helicopter to take her to the hospital. They said that the ride in the ambulance would not be quick enough; she was in critical condition. The helicopter flew her damaged body to the hospital, while my parents drove in their car.

We were sent to my grandmother's house, my mom's mother. Aunt Loretta was there with us as we waited on the phone call about Shell's condition. We were all waiting and crying, and then the phone rang. Aunt Loretta answered the phone—it was my mom. Shell died on the way to the hospital. There was nothing the doctor could do. She was hurt too badly; the car did a lot of damaged to her body.

As we all cried, I thought *where is God*? *Why did my sister have to die? Why not somebody else?* It was the day before Thanksgiving. Just a few hours ago, all I was thinking about was food. Now I would be going to my sister's funeral.

As days went by, my mom cried daily. My dad cried once, and he was never the same. That day took a lot from him. My parents buried my sister about a week later, and the family was never the same. I was saddened and felt even more alone now since Shell was dead. We were very close siblings. Thanksgiving would never be the same; every year when that holiday comes around, we all remember her death.

This is when my dad started to use drugs. He was a good provider, but we did not have a strong father-son relationship. Yes, we did things as a family, but he never came outside to play with my brother or me. Just about every weekend, he would go out with his friends and party. We had food, clothes, and toys for Christmas, but we were disconnected.

We did continue to attend church from time to time. I really did enjoy going to church. Being in church somehow gave me peace, even though I did not understand it. There was something about the way the preacher spoke that caught my attention. I still had an issue with God after losing my sister. I heard the word of God on that Sunday morning, and it was like God Himself was talking to me. His words were penetrating my heart, and I felt convicted. *Jesus,* I said to myself, *where you; who are you*? I was curious about being saved, but he church was not clear to me on how to become saved. I knew within myself I needed a savior. I was thirteen, and I was getting ready to be a freshman in high school the following year.

My mom started to go to a prayer group. The group would assemble every Wednesday night. Members would take turns having a prayer service in their home, but I do not remember ever having prayer service at our house. We did not attend their church, we went to another church, and my dad would talk trash about the pastor and the members.

The pastor's name was Bill Haskins and his wife was Alice. My mom's friend Mrs. Betty Dease introduced us to them. Betty went on Wednesday nights, and one night she took us. Mr. Bill gave me my first real understanding of the Bible, God, and Jesus Christ.

One night during a prayer meeting, I was on my knees and a change came over me.

"You believe, don't you? "asked Pastor Bill Haskins. He had a sparkle in his eye and said it again.

"Yes, I do."

"Alice, get my Bible."

She started reading scriptures to me.

"Do you believe you are sinner?"

"Yes."

"Do you confess with your mouth and believe in your heart that Jesus Christ went to the cross, died, and rose again to live and reign forever?"

"Yes, I do believe that."

"Then you are saved."

It finally happened, and I was excited about my new journey with God. When I went home I told my brother and he laughed at me. My older brother and I were close and just three years apart. He was already planning to leave home to go into the navy. My big brother was my hero. He protected me and defended me, but his response made me feel very bad. I thought he would be happy for me. The next day, I went to school and told Wayne. He could not believe that I did it. It seemed like no one had any faith in me.

My friend named Tina Davis was a classmate and a follower of Christ. She encouraged me and lifted my spirit. She invited me to her church, so I left my family's church. I knew I would not grow there, since most of the congregation was not living according to God's Word. I began going to her church, and I realized there were plenty of young people my age and younger living for Christ. They were not ashamed to say that they were saved. I felt very comfortable and they treated me like family. As months went by, I remained loyal to God and the church. I was seeing a lot of Tina and began to develop a crush on her. We were freshmen in high school, my brother Anthony was preparing to leave home, and I had three younger sisters at home; my life was quickly changing, but I clung to Tina and the church for stability.

Chapter 3

My brother Anthony was a senior and he was getting ready to join the navy. We both loved sports, and the Clemson Tigers were our favorite college football team, but we were divided for the pros: the San Francisco 49ers were my team, but Antony's team was the Miami Dolphins. On Friday nights it was high school football. I had a lot of cousins and friend that played for Swansea High School. Swansea High was well known for football, basketball, and wrestling. Anthony did not play sports in high school, but it was not his fault. He wanted to play, but my dad said no. My dad controlled everything and it was whatever he says goes. He was so busy with his life that he was not part of ours. We all lived in the same house, but there were no connections.

My dad was smoking weed at this time in his life, and after a few months he moved up to snorting cocaine. I saw him with my own two eyes. He had some friends over and, as was the rule when he had company over, we were put up in our rooms until they were gone. I had to use the bathroom, so I peeked into the living room and saw them snorting that white powered drug. My mom did nothing; she just allowed my dad to do whatever. I never knew why my mom put up with that.

Around this time, my dad started to be abusive to my mom. My mom put up with a lot of my dad's mistreatment and abuse, both physical and emotional. He always partied on the weekend while my mom stayed home. He used to come home from drinking and drugging and beat her. She would stay with him regardless. She would not call the cops or report him. One day my dad was slapping my mom around and Anthony went into the room and said, "Daddy, please."

My dad looked at my brother and said, "Go back to your room. This has nothing to do with you. "I think from that day I lost something; I began to doubt God and step away from him.

One day my dad came home with a small baby in his hands. Obviously, we were very curious about this.

"This is Shannon," he said.

Ok, but why was he telling us.

My mom asked whose baby she was, but my dad did not answer. Mom asked about three more times before she began to cry. She was yelling at him, and I knew that baby was his. I thought to myself *how could he bring another baby home to this house? Boy my dad's got some guts doing a thing like that.* After a few more days, things went back to normal. My mom did not leave and my dad continued to be have affairs with different woman. Mom stayed home for us I think. She wanted us to grow up with a father.

Late one night not long after Dad brought Shannon home, we heard some screaming and yelling. Anthony and I looked outside in the back; it was our parents fighting. My dad was really pounding on my mom. Some of the neighbors heard the fight and called my dad's sister. She called my dad's brothers and they came down to stop my dad. My mom was bleeding from the mouth and her clothes were torn. My uncle asked if she wanted to call the police on him, but she said no. Hearing all of the noise, I ventured outside. I asked my dad why he was hitting our mom.

"Junior,"my dad said, "I saw your mom with another man. She was with another man!"

I saw a brick on the ground and my heart was pumping fast. Something in my mind told me to pick up that brick and hit him in the head. *Look what he just did to your mom.* I wanted to hit him so badly, but I did not. *Where is God? Isn't God is supposed to protect us? Why are these things like this?*

Another time, Anthony did something that mom did not like, so she told our dad. When Anthony got home, my dad punched him in the chest and said, "You want to be a man?" After that punch in the chest, Anthony ran in the bathroom to hide. Anthony stayed in the bathroom all night with the door locked to get away from Dad. The next day, Dad just looked at him and Anthony put his head down and went his own way. I thought to myself *that is not going to happen to me.*

It seemed like my life just kept getting worse. I couldn't see God in my life, so I continued to go to church, but not like before. As I went back on God, my thoughts and behavior began to change.

Chapter 3

    Sitting in my room on a Saturday morning, I began to think about all the fun times I have had with my dad. Sometimes we would wake up early and go to the flea market. It was in Springfield about thirty-five minutes from Swansea. We would walk around and look at things. That was fun. He would take us to the professional wrestling matches, since he was a big fan. I thought about the time we went to Myrtle Beach; we stayed in a nice beach house right on the ocean. That was a time I remembered seeing some good in him. *Maybe he is doing the best he knows how to do,* I thought. I wished whatever took control of my dad would let go. I had a good father until the drugs took over. Sitting there in my room, I began to call on the name of Jesus; I knew He would help me. I thought to myself *Jesus is the answer.*

Chapter 4

Walking into the school in the hallways, I would hear people say hurtful things about me and my arms. Some of them thought I was an instrument for their assault. I just wanted to belong to something. Anthony had already graduated and joined the navy by the time I started high school. I was very happy for him, so I signed up to take the military entrance test and I passed. I was going to join the army, but when they recruiter came out to the house and met me, he was shocked. He told me I would never be accepted in the army because of my disability. I was heartbroken. My brother did encourage me to reach for the stars. We still stayed connected even while he was in the navy.

I was still looking for somewhere to belong, but it felt like everyone was overprotective of me because of my arms. My parents would not let me play any sports as a child. I felt like my mom always blamed herself for my condition. She was very protective of me and did not want me to play hard or get hurt. In my own mind, I knew I could compete just like the other kids. I was willing to take a little bodily pain to prove my point. I was already taking the stressful emotional pain—the pain inside they had no idea about.

During my freshman year of high school, I wanted to play football just like my friends. I went to the first three days of practice and I had fun. When I got home that evening, my mother said I had to quit. I was so mad at her and myself; it seemed like I was never going to play any sports like my friends. I thought that if my arms were not short and deformed, she would have let me play.

One day my cousin Rick came over after school while Anthony and I were outside trying to fix our go-cart. He told us about his wrestling match. Being a big wrestling fan since going to matches with my dad, I was very interested. He explained to me the difference between pro and amateur wrestling. My mom wouldn't let me play football, so I thought this could be my chance; I wanted to wrestle too. That was the beginning of a long journey.

I finally convinced my mom to let me try out for the wrestling team my freshman year of high school. Having my brother and cousins on the team really helped me; I guess my mom felt that they would look after me. There was a long line of wrestlers in my family as well. My dad's brother Carson was a high school wrestler at Swansea High School, and was a three-time state champion. We had many other relatives that had wrestled at Swansea High, too. I just wanted a chance to win as well.

You had to be initiated to be on the wrestling team. They ran me down because I tried to run and hold me down. They put creameries or Ben Gay on my testicles. It burned like hell, but I took it and was part of the team. I took mine like a man and lived to fight another day.

Swansea was a very small town, but we wrestled all over the place. We would wrestle schools twice our size and still win. We would practice every day after school for two and half hours. I worked very hard. Wrestling took a lot of work and practice. I was amazed at how strong my teammates were. I couldn't lift as much weight as they could, but what I could lift I did again and again.

I was on top of the world. I loved wrestling. My cousin Elvin Salley was a great help to me. We both trained hard together. When we had wrestling tournament on Saturdays, I would meet Elvin at his house and we would make baloney sandwiches. Then we would walk down to the school to catch the van and go to the wrestling tournament.

My coach's name was Coach Slagel. He gave me the chance to be a part of something special in the wrestling team. Coach Slagel would listen to his country music on every trip we took. He said if we lost, we had to listen to country music on the way home. If we won, we could choose the radio station on the way back home. He was an honest and fair coach; He brought out the best in all of us.

My first season started November 6, 1986 and it ended on February 20, 1987. I remember it like it was yesterday. After all those weeks of practice, it was time for my first match. We were wrestling Orangeburg-Wilkerson High School. That was in Orangeburg South Carolina, about twenty minutes from Swansea. As we arrived I was hyped and pumped up. We all stretched and got loose for about ten more minutes. I had no idea that wrestling would be so hard to learn for me, but I had to find a way to win my matches. Everyone I wrestled already had an advantage over me since my arms were not fully developed and I was not as strong as someone with regular arms.

You had to wrestle the person that weighed the same amount as you. There were thirteen weight classes running from 98 lbs. to 280 lbs. The matches went from the lightest to the heaviest, so I was always first to wrestle because I was 98 lbs. The boy I wrestled for my first match was very strong. He grabbed me and threw me to the mat. In the back of my mind I said *what am I going to do?* I remembered what we did in practice, and it worked. We wrestled three periods for two minutes each. It was 3 to 4 in the last period, and I was losing. I reached down with all my strength and slammed him to the mat. My opponent was on his back, and I was holding him down to get the pin. In the last fifty seconds I pinned him. I jumped up and yelled. My opponent got up, we shook hands, and the referee raised my hand in the air to signal that I won the match. I ran off the mat to my teammates as they congratulated me in my victory. Despite all of my physical differences, I had won the very first wrestling match I ever entered.

As my first season went along, I did not win too many more matches. My arms were my downfall, but I was determined to finish the season. I needed to get stronger and smarter to win more of my matches, so I trained with more experienced and stronger wrestlers. I got a busted lip and I injured my back, but it was well worth it. During my first year, I qualified for the state tournament in the 98-pound weight class. I learned that this was the toughest tournament in the state of South Carolina; boys from all over the state competed in the tournament. I wrestled a boy named James Creech in the first round, but I just couldn't take him, and he went on to win the championship. James was the best wrestler at my weight class at the time. He was strong smart and tough. I wanted to pattern some of my wrestling style like his. He was a winner and never cheated. He won fair and square. I knew that if I wanted to be Champion I had to defeat him one day. I knew every year we would be in the same weight class to wrestle. For the next 3 years it was going to be a battle between him and I. The road to my championship lead straight to James Creech. I was determined that my time was going to come. I had to be ready . I was now the hunter and James was my prey. I sat and cheered my teammates on. I learned more about technique by watching my them, so as we left the tournament I was confident that I was coming back to win the state championship.

Chapter 5

My dad did not come to any of my wrestling matches in all four years. My dad was too busy parting with other women and getting high. He was very selfish. I always wanted my dad to come see me wrestle, since my teammates' dads came to see them wrestle. The other fathers that came rooted for me as well and supported me like I was their own son. My mom did not have a driver's license, but could drive a little. When I had a home match at Swansea High School, she would pack my sisters in the car and drive to the school. After the match I would drive the car home because I had my driver's license. Our prayer group's pastor's son was on the wrestling team. The Pastor supported us 100%, and even traveled with us. I had a lot of support at the matches, but I always wanted to see my dad in stands.

My best friend, Wayne, was on the wrestling team with me. He was like a brother to me. We did everything together, like going to the varsity football games, dating girls, playing sports, even getting into trouble. Wayne treated me with respect and dignity like a true brother. We had a club called "The Boss men" with Elijah, Eric Williams, Herbert, Fredrick Sistrunk, Gus James, John Mack, Dale Gleaton, and Sam Colter aka Nat. We were a tight knit group—brothers to the end. The boss men took turns bringing candy to school. We all had a designated day to bring candy. We all had classes together and gym as well. We had a strong bond between us, and still do to this day.

Wayne's mom is a second mom to me. I was always there, and Wayne was always at my house. Thelma fed me, nurtured, me and loved me like a son. She instructed me, chastised me disciplined me as a son. Here mom Azalea was like a grandma to me. Wayne was her grandson, and so was I. She kept an eye on us all the time. She made sure we were in church and stayed out of trouble. I thank the Lord for them being in my life. I had a big time crush on Wayne's Aunt Francis Wannamaker. To me she was fine and divine—light skin, long hair, and a big smile. She was always friendly and had a calm spirit. She was always nice to me and showed me respect. It was a silly boyhood crush, but I was convinced I wanted to marry her.

Not everyone was as supportive, and I had to learn the hard way that some people would judge me by how I looked. Wayne and Herbert had jobs, and I wanted one too. I heard that Winn-Dixie was hiring baggers, so I managed to get a ride to fill out the application. I talked to the manager, but he said they didn't have any more positions. My friend John walked in as I was leaving to apply for the same position, and he was hired on the spot. The manager had given me one look, and he decided I could not do the job. So many people saw "I can't" stamped on my forehead.

Overall, I had fun in high school. I had teachers who impacted my life. My English teacher Mr. Estridge was a great help. He helped my friends and me with grammar and race relations. He always listened to us and prepared us for the next level in life. We joked around in class, but he had a way of putting us back on track. My teacher Mr. Branham taught us in Deca in the classroom class room . It had an impact in my life as well. We learned about money, checks, account balances and the market of supply and demand. He was funny and let us be ourselves. We cracked jokes on him and he cracked jokes back on us. He taught us to be men and prepared us for the future. We were bless by his teaching and forever transformed in to men of action. My home economics teacher Mrs. Thompson was lady of action and wit. Mrs. T taught us how to cook, sew, and clean—basic life skills I use to this day. We went to conventions with her and learned a lot. She treated us like we were her sons. You can only take her course for two years while in high school, and I tried to take it for three and got kicked out of her class. My friends and I loved Mrs. T. She was the beginning of hope for us, and she took us under her wing.

I started gaining confidence and talking to more girls. There was a girl name Peggy Walker, my friend Dale Gleaton's cousin. Peggy was in the 8th grade, so were just friends since I was older than she was. I did have a crush on our neighbors' daughter Kim Smith. Kim lived next door with her parents and sisters. She was my girlfriend at the time. We would talk sometimes, but that was it. She never treated me badly, not one time. Even though my social life was getting better, I was more concerned about how I would perform on the mat.

The next season in 1987-1988, I was in the tenth grade and wrestling in the 105-weight class. At the beginning of the season, I trained hard. I had one year of experience under my belt, and I was up for the challenge. For some reason, I was having a bad season. I was winning a lot of matches, but I was also losing a lot too. Again, I lost to James Creech. As the season went on I got weak, and I did not qualify for the state championship, but James Creech won again.

I was so disappointed; I cried all night long. I felt like I was not good enough to wrestle. I thought it was my year to win the championship. I thought I had what it took to win, but I had failed. I was standing alone in my room and looking in the mirror. As I sat down on the bed, I thought *I have two more years to win a state championship*. It was summer time, so I had a lot of time to think about what I did wrong. I wanted to get myself straight. I knew that I had a lot to work on; working on my moves and other techniques would help me. Looking back on my season, I saw what I did wrong.

I knew that God was my answer to winning a state championship. I realized that I was a winner no matter what. My mind was made up that I was perfect just the way I was. Being deformed really changed my life—it made me strong. I always had to prove myself to people. At one time I felt so bad about my arms that I would wear long-sleeved shirts everywhere I went. I did not want to show my arms in public at all. Wrestling in front of over 400 people a week changed that. When I went to my matches, people would stare at me. I learned that people were going to look at me regardless, so I opened up. God taught me that He loved me, and that was enough for me. My girlfriend at the time, Peggy Walker, was a very special person who gave me the support and courage to be the best and trust in God.

During the season my junior year I wanted to be like the other guys on the team. Wrestling was a tough sport, so I started to lift weights. I ran about two miles a day to train. The Lord blessed my team with a good season. We won twenty-three matches and lost three matches for the season. Going into the state tournament, I was a fourth-seed wrestler, meaning I was at the bottom. There were eight people in each weight class, so that meant I was going to have my work cut out for me. Luckily, I had people around me who knew all about wrestling and could help me. My cousin Tommy Smith, Roslyn Walker, the Sutton boys, Toby, Moe, Carl Green, Stevie Hallman, Magarrett Simmons, Bill Barry. Tarus Smith, Kevin Simmon, Elvin Salley were all wrestlers. Wayne's uncle was a two-time state champion, and my Uncle Carson was a state champion as well. My brother, cousins, friends, and neighbors all wrestled; they were my support team and helped train me in the wrestling room. Swansea had a tradition of wrestling champions, and I wanted to be part of it. I saw all the trophy and fame, prestige and attention, and I wanted it. I was willing to train hard, work hard, and earn my way to the title of state champion. There was one thing haunting me: James Creech. He was the state champion two years in a row. I knew if I wanted to be the best, I had to beat the best. He was my nightmare at the time. I had already lost to him two years in a row. I needed something more than myself to win.

It was a Friday night in the motel room where we were preparing for the state tournament on Saturday. Coach Siegel began to break down our brackets. He started with me; he said ,"You've got it hard." I had made it to the state championship in last place. My first match was the first-seed wrestler. He was a returning state champion from last year, so the ball was in my court. I went back to my hotel room thinking to myself *this is it; now is the time.* I sat on my bed dreaming, thinking about my life up to now and all the things that brought me here: the pain, heartache, smiles and training, plus the prayers.

Can I really do it and when this thing, or will I just end up a loser? Well I was born with deformed arms. People never gave me a chance my whole life. In the back of their minds, some of them thought I could not be a champion or anything else. I came from a poor family; we did not have much. How could I overcome this big obstacle that was in my way? I was the last seed in the tournament. No one really counted on me to make it in the first place. What am I going to do? In a few hours it would be time for some action.

Growing up handicapped, as they would say, was terrible. No one knew deep inside what the teasing and bullying was doing to me. It was a heavy load to carry. Will I let that distract me from my goal of being state champion? I did not want to let my team down, or myself for that matter. I was determined to win at all costs, no matter what. This might be my last time to get back to this tournament. Losing was not an option for me; it was all or nothing. I knew that is was going to be tough and unpredictable. No matter what, I decide for myself to go all the way. I mean, if other people could win, why not me? Some were bigger, stronger, and even smarter, but I had heart in my favor. That was my point: to show everyone that I was as good as they were. I imagined themcalling my name out as the winner. It was up to me to dig deep down and ask for help.

All my help came from the Lord, Christ Jesus. The will to go all the wayand get the job done came from my faith in the name of Jesus Christ. It began to get late and I knew I needed to get some sleep. I talked to my roommates and began to laugh. I knew I had to wrestle like I had never wrestled before. People were betting on me to lose, which made me more determined than ever. Growing up, people said there were things I just could not do. They did not give me a chance to show if I could do it. Wrestling gave me the chance I always wanted. No help at all—just me and the other person on the mat. I kept saying to myself, *you know can do it.* I knew it would be my day to make history. *Time to get some sleep and be a legend tomorrow.*

Chapter 6

For my first match, I had to wrestle a returning state champion from the previous year, from another weight class. He was in a different weight class last year. He moved up the following year to my weight class and I won. For my second match, I had to wrestle a state runner-up, and I beat him too. That meant I made it to the finals. It also meant that I had James Creech waiting for me as well. James also won his first two matches. I was ready and pumped up. We would have a break before our championship match.

After the break, I was ready; my teammates were yelling and screaming. The whole gym was going crazy. We were in Greenville, South Carolina at Greenville High School. As they called both of our names out, I was very nervous. This was it: I was finally going to wrestle James Creech. We both got on the mat, and we went at it as the whistle blew. We had three rounds of two minutes to wrestle. James threw me, and I threw him. As the match went on, we were tied and time was running out. We were like twins on the mat wrestling each other. When time expired, we were tied up with six points apiece. We had to go into overtime. Both of us were exhausted, sweating and breathing hard. Just into overtime, James threw me hard on the mat and I landed on my left knee. The referee stopped the match. I was in so much pain, but I wanted to continue. The referee asked if I wanted to stop the match, but all I could think was that if they stop the match, I would lose. Oh no; I wanted to win I wanted to be the champion. "Keep going," I said to the referee.

I was limping around the mat trying to stop James from hurting me worse. I managed to score two points to tie the score 8 to 8 at the end of the period, so we were headed into double overtime. I was in pain and sweating badly, but I told my teammates during the break that I would win this match. The whistle blew—time to finish what I started. We both shook hands and grabbed each other. We went back and forth, pushing each other, and then I fell. I could not get up, and the referee stopped the match. He said, "Son, you are hurt and you cannot continue."

As I looked in the other corner, I saw James smiling; he thought it was over. I said, "Give me 30 seconds." I could barely walk. I called one of the other wrestlers from another team. He was close to me with tape in his hand to wrap up my sore knee. Limping toward the mat with my taped-up knee, I looked up at the clock: the score was 8 to 8 with 10 seconds left. At that time I started to pray. *Lord I need your help and your strength.*

I made it back on the mat, the whistle blew, and I managed to grab him and take him down—that gave me two points. I knew that he would get two points if he got up. Aching with pain and exhausted, I held him down, looked up, and started to pray. *Help me hold this boy down, Lord.* James was trying with all his power to get up, but he could not manage to. All I heard was, "5, 4, 3, 2, 1, 0," then the bell went off.

I was the winner of the match. I dropped to my knees and said, "Thank you, Lord!" I was the 112lb State Wrestling Champion. As we both left the mat, we shook hands and hugged. I jumped into the arms of my teammates. I told the other wrestlers on the team, "Go get yours; I got mine!" At the end, we ended up winning the whole tournament as a team. We were the South Carolina High School State Wrestling Champions. At the end of the tournament, they called my name out as the MVP of the state tournament. I was so surprised and ran out to receive my reward. I was a low-seed wrestler and did the impossible. I beat the best of the best. We went on celebrating and having fun. When the wrestling team got back from the state tournament, it was wild. I did not know what to expect from my teammates or classmates., but they treated me like I was king or something. I could not believe my eyes. I was very proud and said *thank you Jesus*. When I started I was last, now the Lord has put me on top. I knew all along I could do it, but I needed to add the main ingredient: Jesus Christ.

Chapter 7

I really studied the bible and ask God to train me in his word. I was under a Pastor at a Local church in Pelion S.C. I had to live right before God and went to a lot of church service some time twice on Sundays. I really wanted God to use me in special way. I gave my all to transcend into a clay to be mold by God. Praying seeking God's will for my life. The Lord had to break me down so he could build me up. I t was not a easy task. I was a reach undo and a sinner before God. I ask the Lord Jesus Christ to come into my heart and forgive me of my sins and be my Lord and Savior. There was a assignment God had for me. But I had to be taught the Lords way. Forgiveness and repentance. Once I submitted to his ways I was moving forward in Life, Kingdom Building. I was very hunger for the presence of the Lord .Eight years later I was a youth leader in church and spoke on Youth Sunday. I enjoyed going to church and praising God. After a few years I walked away. I was teased about preaching and serving God. I was preaching on the street corner and in church. I let people talk me out of it. I started going out and drinking and smoking weed. I was fornicating with woman; I was a hot mess. I hooked up with a guy writing bad checks all over town. I got arrested and served six months in county jail. While I was in jail, I started reading my Bible and doing Bible study. Before I was released, I was the head of our Bible study. I got out went back with a lady who's using drugs and staying out late. I was not happy. I still was barely going to church.

Then one night I was outside behind the high school gym, and I began to talk to God. I said, "Lord I am tired and I want a change in my life. I want more out of life." I asked the Lord to help me get back to the point where I loved him the most. I asked Him to help me live holy and be holy. I wanted a fresh start. My brother was in Ohio at the time, so I called him and he said I could go live with him. My heart said go and start over with a new life, even though I was still attached to this lady name Cassandra and street life. Cassandra and I had a brief relationship and it was not a healthy one at that. That was not what God pick for me, I picked that messed up relationship.

I went to my aunt's house and packed up. I told my cousin Alicia I was leaving to go to Ohio, but she didn't believe me. I packed my clothes in a trash bag and got my ticket to Ohio; the next day I left Swansea. The bus trip was great. I rode along and talked to God, asking Him to help me start over.

I got off the bus in twenty-two hours at my brother's wife's house, where I was going to stay while they were separated. I got a job working at B.J Allan, a place where they make fireworks.

I met a guy named Will and we became friends. I had to adjust to new people, because they had never seen someone like me before with my disability with my deformed arms. At first, it was hard all over again. *Here we go again,* I thought, *all the staring and explaining about my arms.*

I had a friend name Helen who worked at the same place as I did. I asked her out, and she said yes. I really liked her, but she just used me for my time and money and what I could do for her. She had other men on the side. I was heartbroken when I found out. I learned my lesson and I moved on.

The pain in my arms was constant. They would ache and I would not tell a soul. I just suffered in pain alone. I want to be near Jesus, but something was in my way. I watched and waited, and now I recognize that He was already there for me. I had to go through a process of letting myself go, to be torn down all the way, physical, emotionally, and spiritually.

As I lay at night in my room, crying myself to sleep, I thought to myself, *is there anyone that feels my pain*? Suddenly, I finally got it; I was chosen to run the race he has put in my path, and to represent Him and the kingdom of God. The love of Jesus filled my heart and took all the pain away, both emotional and physical. I had to go through pain so Jesus Christ could bring me out. The Lord Jesus is perfect in everything, even when we think he has left us. Jesus is the best thing that ever happened to me. He gave his life to rescue me. It is clear to see that I will never be same. I give Him glory and honor; all the praises belong to him. Be encouraged, and let the Lord free you from sin and death. Give your life to Jesus Christ today not tomorrow. I know who I belong to and represent (John 3:16). The Lord helps me to be just like you: to love and forgive, be helpful in every way, live a life pleasing the Father in heaven.

Chapter 7

Then I met Lynnette Stewart one day at work. She was working on the line and I was a sorter. One day she was getting on my nerves complaining about her stock. Then she said, "If I give you something will you use it?" I said yes, and she gave me her phone number. I waited a couple of days, and then I called her. I told her where I was from and she told me she had two little boys, Jalen who was four and Tralen who was two. I always loved kids and wanted to be a dad.

I took her to church with me a couple of times. I was trying to get back straight with the Lord. I was done playing around. Regardless of what decisions I made, I would always find myself in church at the altar. All life experiences, past, present, and future, revolve around my Lord and Savior Jesus Christ. I was chosen by God to do His Will. Now I realize my purpose in life. Sometimes I would sleep over at Lynnette's house, then realized I cannot lay with this woman and not be married.

One night I told her that God had called me to preach his Word, "I wanted to know if you would still be with me."

"Yes," she said, "I will still be with you. Do what God wants you to do."

After five months, I proposed and she said yes. I drove down to Swansea for my mom and dad to meet Lynnette and her kids. We planned a wedding. Her family was already there in Ohio, so I sent for my family to come to Ohio for the wedding. My mom and dad came; my aunts, uncles, cousins, my sisters and brother were all there. Wayne, his girlfriend Katie, and our friend John Mack were there too.

I fell in love with Lynnette's boys and think of them as my own sons. I always wanted children, but I did not want any child to bear my burden. If a child ended up with arms like mine, it would be too hard for me to accept. I did not want that for any child. So the Lord blessed me to be a father without that burden.

After we were married, my ministry began. God has truly blessed us through the years. We have relocated to Charlotte, North Carolina. We are still here on the battlefield for the Lord in ministry. God is an awesome God; He blessed my sister and brother in Christ Jesus.

My wife and I have been married for sixteen years now. Jalen and Tralen are still with us in Charlotte as a family. God was preparing me for my future and I did not even know it. People see me and ask how I can do the things I do. My answer is always *God helped me to do everything I do*. God wanted to get the glory out of my life as a way to show people that God is real and alive. Sometimes I did not want to be chosen because of all the trial and hardship, but then I had to grab hold of myself and remind myself that if God is for me, who can be against me? God has never let me down, and He always keeps all of his promises. Being disabled has taught me a lesson, and I am very grateful for my life.

I want to encourage your hearts and spirits today. God has not forgotten about you. What you see as a curse, God will use that to bless and elevate you to the next level. Trust God at his word and have faith in him. Seek and you shall find; knock and it shall be open to you. You will be empowered and have life more abundantly. Peace will capture your heart and mind with forgiveness. Seek the Lord and walk in holiness and righteousness. The Lord has freed you from your past to launch you into your blessed future. Repent and you shall be saved. We are still living, preaching and teaching God's Holy Word. Get to know God for yourself and love yourself. Believe in yourself, and go for your goals; do not let anyone stop you. You can make your dreams come true and follow your heart. May God bless you and give you peace and wisdom.

Chapter 7

Chapter 7

Elijah Dixon Jr.
816 Justice Avenue
Charlotte, NC 28206
704-605-2405
elijahdixonjr@yahoo.com

www.ingramcontent.com/pod-product-compliance
Lightning Source LLC
LaVergne TN
LVHW081454060526
838201LV00050BA/1797